Made in the USA
Coppell, TX
07 July 2021

58657059R00057